CREATING A COMMUNITY OF PRACTICE

A Guide for Administrative Professionals

By Carol Walsh

Carol Walsh, Copyright

All rights are reserved.

No permission is given for any part of this book to be reproduced, transmitted in any form, or means; electronic or mechanical, stored in a retrieval system, photocopied, recorded, scanned, or otherwise. Any of these actions require the proper written permission of the author.

ISBN: 9798471077256

Published 2022

Special Thanks

A special thank you to Chrissy Scivicque. A former administrative professional and Founder, CEO and Lead Trainer of CCS Ventures, LLC, a training and coaching company specializing in professional development and career advancement. She works with individuals and teams, providing education and support to help elevate workplace performance and increase career satisfaction. Chrissy is also the author of several books.

Thank you, Chrissy, for your support and encouragement to write this book.

Dedication

This book is dedicated to members of the Core Team who shared my vision and worked hard to better the work lives of our administrative professional colleagues.

CREDITS

Images designed by Carol Walsh and produced using Canva.com, License Agreement, Chirp Media.

ACKNOWLEDGEMENT

Achieving More Together is a fictitious name of the community of practice I reference throughout this book. The experiences shared here, are from true events or situations experienced during my time as the community coordinator.

Many resources used are influenced by products of American Productivity & Quality Center (APQC). APQC is the world's foremost authority in benchmarking, best practices, process and performance improvement, and knowledge management. Although member-base, APQC's does provide public content. APQC remains the world's leader in transforming organizations. Visit us at **www.apqc.org** and learn how you can make best practices your practices.

Contents

Introduction 1
The Power of Communities of Practice 5
Getting Started 9
Cultivating a Successful Community of Practice 15
Understanding the Fundamentals 19
Key Elements 20
The Planning Process 25
Creating a Core Team 33
Foundational Documents 35
Lessons Learned - Building Your Team 38
Engaging Members 43
Membership Engagement Levels 44
Five Approaches to Engagement 46
Keeping the Momentum 57
Refreshing the CoP 59
Scaling and Engaging New Members 61
When is it time? 65
Getting Feedback 67
Monitoring Success 73
Conclusion 85
Appendices 88
References 97

Forward

Written by Queenie Wei - Author and Entrepreneur

There are times when knowledge alone is not enough. What we call performance is based on practicality and that simply means you must be willing to put in the work. But what does that mean exactly?

Carol Walsh is my mother-in-law, although she is already a published author, I know this book is dear to her heart as she has poured her heart and soul into empowering the next generation of administrative professionals.

As a previous Executive Assistant, I didn't realize I actually belonged to a community of practice, the AAP (Association of Administrative Professionals). The community would meet monthly and empower admin professionals from all different industries. We had all sorts of activities and speakers who would come and present to us once a month so that we could learn and expand our own knowledge. Beyond the learning, it provided emotional support for members of the group when we deal with "challenging" scenarios.

What I find most unique about the administrative profession is that we not only manage "work" tasks within the organization but often we ARE the mental and emotional support to the person we are assisting.

Executives count on their admin support to manage important aspects of their work life or personal life.

Imagine carrying out your duties knowing you have a place to turn to when the going gets tough, that is the essence of creating a community of practice.

The concept was first proposed by cognitive anthropologist Jean Lave and educational theorist Etienne Wenger. Carol brings these concepts to life in a way that is both digestible and easy to implement within your current role.

A community of practice is not meant to be the responsibility of a single person but rather an initiative by a cohort of individuals who share the same goals. Individuals who are willing to take that first step into evolving their own admin roles while benefiting the entire organization.

There is no single method that gets you on the path to success. It is an accumulation of actions that you take. You won't find fluff or jargon here, but instead, you'll be learning from her own experiences. She focuses on the elements that will guide you toward your next step.

Often in this type of guidebook, you get a ton of information but no action steps. Each chapter Carol writes is backed by her own as well as equipping you with actionable steps. Perseverance is what you will find at the end of this book. It is a guide, if you are looking to have the work done for you, this is not it. But if you are looking for support and real guidance, I highly recommend you read this book.

Preface

Having worked in the administrative field for the last 30-plus years of my life, I thought I had mastered the practice. But it was not until later in my career that I had the opportunity to both do a deep dive and build a Community of Practice (CoP).

The most rewarding part of my experience is not the work itself but being able to see the value and how the CoP uplifts not only the administrative professionals within our team but how this very practice can push the organization into new levels of growth. This very essence is what I am trying to recreate in these pages and present to you as a steppingstone to try this in your organization.

This book represents my own journey from the failures, successes, and learnings of building and nurturing several Communities of Practice. Throughout this book, I've made a careful effort to share some examples for your reference and sourced all the materials that you may potentially need to be able to create your own.

I hope it can inspire, challenge, and make it simple for you to take that first step into building your very own Community of Practice.

INTRODUCTION

"Alone, we can do so little, together we can do so much." --Helen Keller

As administrative professionals, it is essential that we keep our skills and knowledge up to date. This means attending training courses and seminars on a regular basis. Not only does this keep us sharp, but it also shows our employers that we are committed to our jobs.

In today's competitive job market, it is more important than ever to make sure we are continuously developing our skills. By doing so, we not only improve our chances of getting promoted, but we also make ourselves more valuable to our employers.

Annually the American Society for Administrative Professionals conducts a survey of their members. In 2022, the results reported,

"With the rapid pace of change, both organizations and APs [Administrative Professionals] stand to benefit immensely from identifying needs for upskilling and ongoing training and development, particularly as these roles expand more into strategic initiatives and leadership partnership."

The survey also identified that to be successful our profession it will be necessary to build power skills and technical expertise.

The report went on to alert hiring managers, the administrative profession is increasingly becoming a very competitive landscape for hiring talent in this field.

It has been widely accepted that employees who have access to learning opportunities are more engaged and have higher job satisfaction than those who do not. However, in many organizations, access to learning opportunities is limited, which creates a barrier for employees. In order to understand why this is the case, it is important to first understand what learning opportunities are. Learning opportunities are defined as any chance for an individual to learn new information or skills. This can include formal education, such as college courses or professional development seminars, as well as informal learning, such as reading articles or watching webinars.

Research has shown that there are numerous benefits to employees who have access to learning opportunities. These benefits include increased job satisfaction, engagement, and motivation, as well as improved job performance. Additionally, employees who have access to learning opportunities are more likely to stay with an organization for a longer period of time.

Despite these benefits, many organizations still do not provide their employees with access to learning opportunities. There are several reasons for this, including budget constraints and a lack of understanding of the importance of learning opportunities.

However, the most common reason is that organizations simply do not prioritize learning and development. As a result of this, employees are often left to fend for themselves when it comes to finding learning opportunities.

This can be a major barrier, as it can be difficult and time-consuming to find quality learning opportunities on one's own. Additionally, employees may not have the financial resources to pay for courses or seminars out of their pockets.

A barrier like this has left many administrative professionals feeling under-valued, so they become complacent in their roles. A few become leaders, innovators, and collaborators building their support networks on their own.

Lifelong learning is essential for success in today's world. Whether you're looking to advance your career, learn a new skill, or simply stay up to date on current trends, continuing your education is crucial. For many people, traditional education institutions are not the best fit. That's where communities of practice can come in.

I always found myself pondering on ways to discover alternative and ongoing development opportunities. My thoughts kept coming back to the "collective" - together we can achieve more. Maybe there are others who felt the same? Maybe we could make this happen, as the cliché goes, "numbers speak louder than words".

With a little creativity and resourcefulness, and the rest falls into place. Administrative professionals have never been very comfortable engaging with leaders, until recent times. It has always been seen as being best to do your work and not be heard.

This attitude is slowly changing with administrative professionals are more willing to engage with leaders to discuss and collaborate on ways to improve their organizations.

This guide provides administrative professionals with theory, tools, and resources to create a community of practice. Additionally, I will share some of the lessons learned throughout my experience with establishing a CoP.

The community of practice I will reference throughout this book will be known as the Achieving More Together, Community of Practice (CoP). This was established in June 2019 within a large health care organization.

THE POWER OF COMMUNITIES OF PRACTICE

> *"There is no power for change greater than a community discovering what it cares about."*
> *-- Margaret J. Wheatly*

Creating a community of practice takes effort and you want it to be successful. You need to have a clear goal in mind for the community, and make sure all members are on board with it. You'll also need to provide a lot of support and guidance in the early stages until the community is self-sufficient. Finally, you need to be prepared to stick with it for the long haul - a successful community of practice takes time and dedication to grow.

We created a learning community. This was an organic process that unfolded over time. The concept of a CoP is not new. In fact, there are many communities of practice already in existence within organizations. The one we created was unique in that it was a virtual administrative professionals CoP and spanned across the province.

I had the opportunity to work with a group of amazing individuals who were dedicated to their professional development and committed to supporting the initiative. Let me share with you the approaches we used, and lessons learned, so you can create your successful CoP.

Simply put, our goal was to have everyone working from the same foundation of knowledge and skills. In order to accomplish this, we needed to set in place a number of foundational guidance documents, and programs, and identify opportunities for the administrative professionals to come together. The key to the success of any CoP is the members' willingness to share their knowledge and expertise with each other in a safe and trusting environment.

Acknowledging the organization also benefits from a CoP, there are many benefits to members such as:

- Learning from others who have more experience or different skills.
- Sharing best practices.
- Building a network of peers.
- Developing new skills and knowledge.
- Increasing confidence and competence.
- Staying current with trends and changes.

Communities of practice can provide support and encouragement, as well as a wealth of knowledge and resources. It can also help you to focus your efforts and keep you accountable. Most importantly, it provides a place for like-minded individuals to come together and share their passion. So, if you're feeling "stuck in a rut", or simply looking for some inspiration here are a few tips to get you thinking about the CoP you want to build:

Define the purpose and goals. What is the focus of the community? What are the goals?

Identify the members. Who will be involved? How will they be recruited?

Create a structure. How often will it meet? What format will it take? What tools and resources will be used?

Facilitate. Who will lead the discussions? Who will be responsible for creating and maintaining the structure?

Evaluate. How will you know if it is successful? How do you plan to measure performance?

Creating a CoP can be a rewarding experience for both the members and facilitators. It is an opportunity to learn, grow, and build capacity within a group of individuals who are committed to supporting each other. You are the change agents for your organization's administrative professionals.

GETTING STARTED

"...communities of practices are groups of people who share a concern or passion for something they do and learn how to do it better as they interact regularly."
-- Etienne Wegner

As a career administrative professional for more than three decades, I admit I was oblivious to what a CoP was. I heard the term mentioned many times but was truly unaware of the concept and brushed it aside as jargon.

Years later, I was approached to create one. I started asking questions, "What would that mean for us? "How does someone create a CoP?" It was apparent I did not understand the concept. Curiously, I set out to discover what the term *"Community of Practice"* was all about; what were they talking about? Allow me to share my learnings with you.

Aware of journal clubs, associations, discussion groups and the like but never the term "community of practice". Etienne and Beverly Wenger-Trayner are the pioneers of the CoP concept. Etienne Wenger believes organizations that encourage, support, and sponsor communities of practice enjoy the benefits of their work. In essence, the groups mentioned above were in fact communities of practice.

For administrative professionals, CoPs have existed on an informal basis and often in a meeting setting. Communities of practice can be seen as a support system where people come together to share interests, abilities, and knowledge. By working together, they can define and organize processes, set best practices for common work across the organization, create opportunities for the team to become more effective and efficient, and collectively, influence how they work. This sounds like something that administrative professionals have been doing in group meetings for a long time. In addition, CoPs can encompass others outside of your immediate area. Wouldn't it be great to have this type of support and opportunity in the workplace?

Administrative professionals are the foundation of any organization. Management is responsible for ensuring they are supported, capable of performing their duties and have the confidence to meet ever-changing roles and responsibilities. A CoP helps to achieve this and is the right fit within any organization.

In an earlier role, I witnessed other disciplines are offered ongoing educational opportunities. I am certain this is commonplace, but I couldn't help asking, "why did my fellow admins not attend conferences or other training sessions?"

Management's response was always, "we don't have the budget". What we really heard was "as an admin you would not get the financial support to attend" or "you wouldn't get the time off work." It was all on your dime

I approached the Chief Executive Officer (CEO) to ask why administrative professionals were not being given these same opportunities. The response could have been interpreted as "admins do not have the same return on investment or value other disciplines would". However negative sounding the response was, it drove me to push the issue. The CEO suggested that if I could find a way that did not cost money, they could support ongoing education for this group. It did not really answer the inequity question, but at least I had them listening.

Reaching out across the organization, I connected with subject matter experts to deliver sessions. A roster was developed, and with a plan in hand, I made a presentation to our Leadership team. They accepted the proposal; we were on our way. I did not know it at the time and reflecting now, it was a community of practice. This was a temporary fix - short-lived and not a lot was achieved as interest and support dwindled. Some opportunities evolved, and it was a start.

What does a CoP do?

When I discovered the diagram[1] that follows on the next page, I feel it really reflects what a community of practice is about. My high-level interpretation suggests that a CoP breaks down barriers (challenges) and approaches these challenges with a solution-focused and results-driven approach.

This diagram on the next page exemplifies why CoPs are created.

---

[1] This diagram was a pencil drawing by an unknown author. It was recreated by Carol Walsh, 2022.

CoPs can help organizations achieve their goals by providing support and opportunities for members to become more effective and efficient.

A member of the CoP once shared her reflections about a community of practice in that they are safe and trusting environments. The openness to hearing the ideas of others and collectively solving problems together. Another key observation she reflected on, were the silos that occur in organizations and how they can be damaging and frustrating hindering effective communication and collaboration.

As she became more actively involved, she witnessed first-hand how CoPs are a way to break down barriers and fosters appreciation for how others work making it easier to work across the organization.

The benefits acquired through a CoP are many. To name a few; some experience increased job satisfaction and motivation, improved communication, and collaboration, as well as increased knowledge sharing and innovation. Administrative professionals become better equipped to meet the needs of their roles.

A CoP provides a space for admins to connect with others who may have gone through similar challenges. It is a place to share best practices and learn from each other. To be successful, a CoP requires dedication and commitment from its facilitators and members. The payoffs can be great, but only if the members are willing to put in the work.

Are you part of a community of practice? If not, why not start one? Admins are often the glue that holds an organization together. Administrative professionals are the problem-solvers and the go-to people. They are always seeking ways to improve and be more efficient. Why not do so through a CoP and tap into the collective knowledge of your fellow admins?

The next chapter will speak to the nuances of a community of practice and how to cultivate your CoP.

CULTIVATING A SUCCESSFUL COMMUNITY OF PRACTICE

"I alone cannot change the world, but I can cast a stone across the waters to create many ripples."
-- Mother Teresa

Communities of practice can be found in all sorts of industries, disciplines from business to education, to even the arts. What they have in common is that they are all places where people can exchange ideas, learn new skills, and build relationships. Each one will be slightly different from another.

The key to creating a successful community of practice is to design for evolution. Meaning, creating a structure that can accommodate new members, new ideas, and new ways of doing things. It also means being open to different perspectives and inviting different levels of participation.

Creating a community of practice can be a difficult task, but it is possible to create a successful community by following these seven principles. I will present more detail on these principles in the coming pages.

One way to create a CoP that is both familiar and exciting is to focus on value. What can members of the community get from participating? What can they learn from each other? How can they make a difference in the workplace? When people come together around a shared purpose, they are more likely to create something that is truly valuable.

Another way to ensure that a community of practice is successful is to create a rhythm for the community. This might involve regular meetings, online forums, or other forms of communication. Whatever the method, it is important to have a way for members to stay in touch and keep the community alive.

By focusing on value and creating a rhythm for the community, you can ensure that your community of practice is successful. The following principles[2] will help guide your success as a CoP.

> **Focus on value.** This means that the community should be focused on creating and sharing value, rather than simply exchanging information. The community should also be open to new members who can contribute to the community's goals.
>
> **Create a rhythm for the community.** Having a regular schedule or other activity that keeps members engaged creates a rhythm. For example, monthly education sessions. The community should also have a way to communicate outside of meetings, such as through an online forum, newsletter, or simply reaching out to other members.

---

[2] Principles of Communities of Practice, Etienne Wenger, Richard McDermott, and William M. Snyder, MBS Working Knowledge, 2002

Community is Accessible. The community should be open to anyone who wants to join as long as those fit within the parameters of the CoP. It should be easy for members to find information and resources. The community should also be aware of the different levels of expertise of its members and make sure that everyone feels welcome.

Promote Learning. The community should provide opportunities for members to learn from each other and from experts. The community should also encourage members to share their knowledge with others.

Design for evolution. Creating a structure that can accommodate new members, new ideas, and new ways of doing things will satisfy the growth and evolution of a CoP. It is important to be open to change and to allow the community to grow and evolve over time.

Foster Collaboration. Inviting different people with unique backgrounds and experiences to participate in the CoP brings a variety of viewpoints to create a well-rounded and successful CoP.

The CoP should encourage members to support each other to solved problems, create new ideas, and resources. To cultivate and maintain a successful CoP, it is important to focus on creating and sharing value, having a regular rhythm, being open and accessible, promoting learning, designing for evolution, and fostering collaboration. These principles will help create a CoP that is focused on the goals of the group and provides support and resources for its members.

UNDERSTANDING THE FUNDAMENTALS

"Practice is a shared history of learning. Practice is conversational. 'Communities of Practice' are groups of people who share a concern (domain) or a passion for something they do and learn how to do it better (practice) as they interact regularly (community)."
-- *Etienne Wenger*

Before we get into setting up a CoP, we need to understand some of the fundamentals first. Communities of practice are groups of people who share a common interest or goal and come together to collaborate and learn from each other. CoPs can exist in any industry or field, and membership can be open to anyone with the appropriate skills or knowledge.

One of the key benefits of belonging to a CoP is access to the collective intelligence of the group. Members can learn new skills and find solutions to problems they wouldn't be able to solve on their own. CoPs also provide an opportunity for networking and building relationships with other professionals.

There are four key elements of a CoP: **purpose, working together, continuous learning, and support of practice.** When professionals work together, the sharing of ideas and resources seems easier, and continuous learning improves the quality of the work.

KEY ELEMENTS

The term "community of practice" has become increasingly popular in recent years, particularly in a learning organization. A community of practice can be distinguished from a more general "community" in that it is a purposeful group with a shared domain of interest. In other words, members of a community of practice are united by a common goal or interest, and they interact with one another in order to further that goal. I will share what I have learned about these key elements in the coming pages.

Key Elements of a CoP, Carol Walsh, 2022

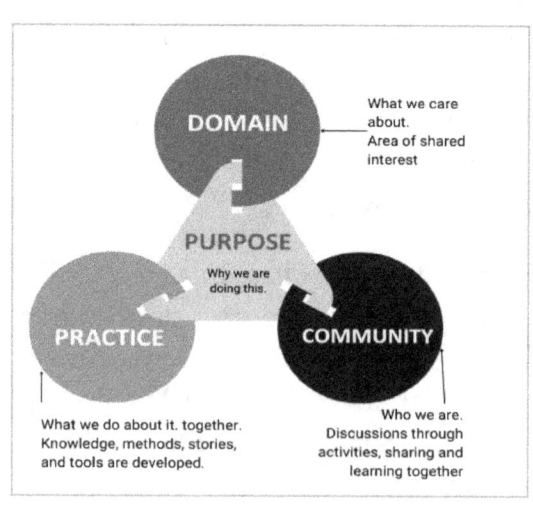

The intersection of community and domain in practice is an important one, as it is through this juncture that learning and professional development take place. Let's take a few minutes to discuss the key elements:

Purpose: A CoP needs to have a clear purpose that outlines why it exists and what its members hope to achieve. Without a purpose, a community of practice will struggle to connect members and guide their activities.

Working Together (Community): One of the key benefits of a CoP is the ability for members to easily share ideas and resources. When professionals work together, they can pool their knowledge and expertise to solve problems more effectively.

Continuous Learning (Practice): A CoP should be focused on continuous learning so that its members can keep up with the latest best practices and trends. Continuous learning helps to improve the quality of the community of practice's work and keeps members engaged.

Support (Domain): Effective communities of practice need the support of organizational leaders to function properly. Leaders can provide resources, promote collaboration, and remove barriers to participation. Without leadership support, a CoP is likely to struggle.

One of the organizations I worked in was spread across the entire province, had more than 100,000 employees and a unionized environment which presents its own challenges.

Many administrative professionals reported they felt isolated but safer in their silos. Little to no communication with other admins, even sometimes outside their own unit within their own team. They expressed challenges they were facing and felt that they had no support. Some were okay with working within the silos.

It was management driving the call to action to create a community of practice. They emphasized the need to strengthen the administrative team by building capacity, competency, and confidence to address the challenges they were facing. Our call to action – "build capacity amongst administrative professionals".

The Achieving More Together CoP was the first CoP for administrative professionals in my organization. Many healthcare organizations have many types of communities found amongst healthcare professionals such as nurses, physiotherapists, speech pathologists, educators to list a few - nothing for admins.

As mentioned previously, a community of practice needs to have a clear purpose. The statement needs to provide direction and support the existence of the CoP. When setting up your CoP, think about what the community of practice's intent is.

What do you hope to accomplish with it? The response may be a call to action, or simply to provide support for its members. For example, your purpose could be: *"to provide professional development sessions to administrative professionals in our organization."*

By building a professional network of cross-boundary relationships, our CoP has evolved. We aim to ensure administrative professionals have the skills and knowledge required to excel in their jobs and are part of a mutual support network that contributes to success at work.

Few organizations have dedicated employees to support communities of practices and their work. Typically, communities do not have paid staff to coordinate their activities. It has been my experience that not having or recognizing dedicated support/coordination creates a barrier restricting the size of the membership. We limited the intake because we were working off the side of our desk and still needed to maintain our regular duties. A small team would be coordinating the activities, so we wanted to keep it manageable. After completing major initiatives over the first two years, we began to open our membership to other portfolios. By year three, we added another portfolio. The scale and spread had begun. I offer more on this activity later in the book.

The Planning Process

"If you don't know where you are going, you'll end up someplace else." -- Yogi Berra

We often refer to a "launch" as an event to start something like a new program, project, or initiative. The same applies to building a CoP right up to showcasing it to its target audience.

Building a thriving community of practice takes time and effort, but it is worth it when done correctly. The first step is to define the purpose and goals of the community, which will help determine who should be involved, what kind of content to share, and how to measure success. After that, it is important to choose the right platform and set up the structure of the community.

Then comes the difficult part - identifying and engaging potential members. Once they are on board, it is time to start creating and curating content. This content should be relevant to the community's goals and interests, and it is important to market and promote the community so that others can find it and get involved. Finally, it is important to constantly evaluate and adjust the community as needed to ensure its success.

Our CoP combined models and found this method below contributed to our success. Allow me to provide additional details about each step in this process.

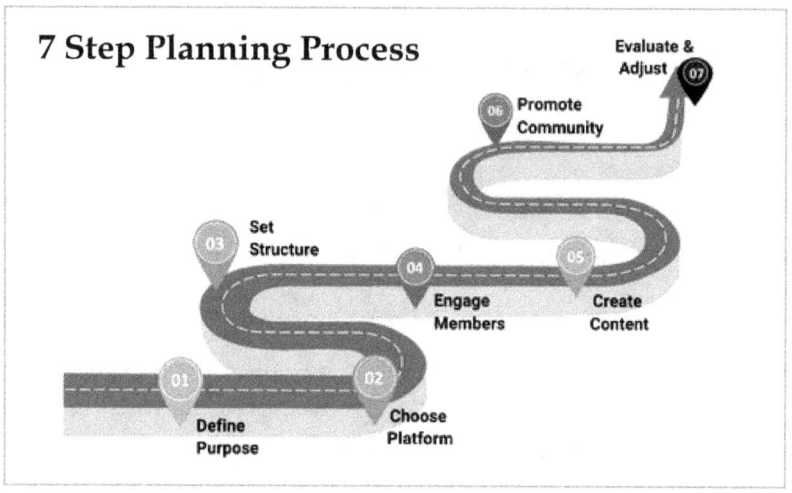

Source: 7 Step Planning Process, Carol Walsh, 2022

Define the purpose and goals of the community: The first step is to define the purpose and goals of the community clearly. Doing this will help you determine who should be involved, what kind of activities and content to share, and how to measure success.

Choose the right platform: Make sure you have the correct tools in place to support your community of practice. There are many great platforms out there, so do your research and pick the one that fits. For example, the CoP I reference throughout used a SharePoint platform, some may use an internal web interface. There are some CoPs who actually have their own domain on an external web service.

Set up the structure: Now that you know what you want to achieve, it is time to set up the structure of your community of practice. This includes creating rules and guidelines, appointing moderators, and deciding on a format for content.

Identify and engage potential members: The next step is to identify and engage potential members who will form the committee, recruit new members, and assist with onboarding.

Create and curate content: Creating and curating your content is the next step. This includes developing a content strategy, creating original content, and curating external content.

Promote and grow the community: It is necessary to promote and grow the CoP. This includes marketing the CoP, encouraging participation, and moderating content. Make sure everyone knows about your new CoP! Use social media, email lists, and other channels to get the word out.

Evaluate and adjust as needed: The final step is to evaluate and adjust as needed. This includes setting goals, measuring success, and making changes to improve the community of practice. This may include adding new features, changing the structure, and improving content.

Building the Structure

"To be part of a family, or a community, is to have duties and responsibilities, to be bound by rules of that group." -- Robin Hobb

To create a successful community, you should determine the key roles and responsibilities of the leadership that will guide the activities. A sample structure is provided below followed by a brief description of roles and responsibilities supporting a well-structured CoP. Highly recommending a formal structure like this in unionized environments.

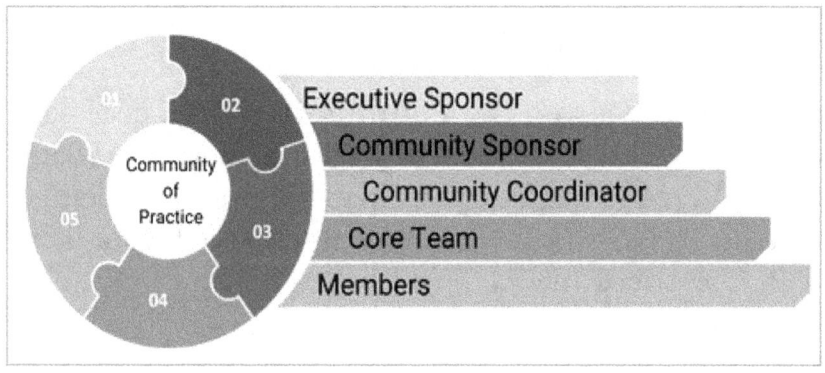

Source: Sample CoP Structure, Carol Walsh, 2022

Community of Practice Champion or Executive Sponsor: The role of a Community of Practice Champion or Executive Sponsor is to ensure the CoP has the support it needs from management, to communicate the purpose of the community to its members, and to promote the CoP within the organization.

They work to ensure impact within the organization, share the community's contributions of practice to the formal organization and enable organization support of the CoP. Ensuring support from management is critical to the success of a CoP. The champion should ensure that there is a valid purpose behind the CoP and that it has the support it needs from management to succeed.

Communicating the purpose of the CoP is also important. The champion should ensure members understand the goals of the community and what they can expect to get out of it. They should also promote the CoP within the organization so that more people are aware of it and its benefits.

Finally, the champion should work to ensure impact within the organization. This may include communicating the contributions of the CoP to the formal organization and promoting organization support for the community. By doing this, the champion can help to make sure that the community has a lasting impact on the organization.

Community of Practice Sponsor: The Community of Practice Sponsor's role is to support the CoP and act as a bridge between the CoP and the rest of the organization. In addition, the sponsor facilitates communication, manages official relationships, and removes any barriers that may prevent the CoP from being productive.

The Sponsor is instrumental in establishing the mission and the expected outcomes for the CoP. Community of practice members are recruited for their expertise relevant to the practice or strategic services. They participate in discussions, raise issues and concerns regarding every day needs and requirements, alert other members to any changes in conditions and requirements, are on the lookout for ways to enhance CoP effectiveness (e.g., by recruiting high-value members) and above all, they learn.

Community of Practice Coordinator: The community of practice coordinator facilitates group discussion to ensure appropriate and respectful communication. They develop the agenda and/or objectives for the subsequent CoP meeting and send out regular messages to all CoP members about the next meeting/activity. Unless otherwise agreed, any costs arising from activities under the CoP will be at the member or participant's expense and may be subject to available funds, personnel, and other resources unless a budget has been provided. The coordinator sits on all committees, working groups, and project teams as an ad hoc member in an advisory capacity.

Webmaster: The webmaster is responsible for maintaining and updating the CoP website content. This may include developing or sourcing new content, as well as ensuring that all existing content is accurate and up to date. The webmaster also liaises with the CoP coordinator to ensure that all relevant information is distributed to CoP members promptly and effectively. Each committee, working group and project team may choose to identify a webmaster for their group.

Facilitator: The facilitator's role is to make sure the CoP discussion runs smoothly. Each committee, project team and working group will have a facilitator who assumes the group's leadership position. They are responsible for developing the agenda and/or objectives for the meeting sending out regular messages to all CoP members about the next meeting/activity and ensuring that communication is respectful and appropriate.

Chapter Site Coordinator: Chapter sites within a CoP usually surface when there may be a need for specialization or there are several people who share an interest and want to branch off on their own but remain under the umbrella of the bigger CoP. These chapter sites operate independently.

The responsibilities of the Chapter Site Coordinator include managing chapter members, maintaining the chapter website, coordinating regular meetings, and documenting processes, to name a few. The site administrator will also represent the chapter at the Core Team level and assign representatives to sit on the various committees, working groups and project teams for the overall activities of the CoP.

Obtaining Sponsorship

> "...sponsorship can make a huge impact on the CoP's success and leverage." [3] -- *Fontaine and Prusak*

---

[3] Keeping communities of practice afloat: Understanding and fostering roles in communities, Fontaine and Prusak

A sponsor is an individual or group that provides resources and support to a CoP. The resources can be financial, knowledge-based, or networking-related. The level of involvement can vary from being an active participant to simply lending their name to the group. In return, the sponsor can expect increased visibility within the organization, improved employee morale and motivation, and an overall increase in innovation.

When looking for a sponsor, it is important to identify someone who shares the same values as the CoP and is passionate about its success. The sponsor does not need to be a subject matter expert, but they should be willing to champion the group and its activities.

The support received from the sponsor can vary in level of support. You may have more than one sponsor who actively participants and supports the activities of your CoP. Other sponsors are only involved from an awareness perspective.

Many CoPs operate without formal sponsors. Others may need formal approval for resource allocation and the type of services offered. For example, if involvement in the CoP is during work time, seek leadership support. Discussing with your leadership about the role and what it might involve will determine if you need one.

Sponsors can legitimize the CoP and help attract members. They can also help find needed expertise for community members and promote the CoP's outcomes across organizational boundaries. Additionally, they can act as liaisons between the CoP and other levels of leadership and tie the community and its benefits to the organization's strategic goals.

Finally, sponsors can measure and evaluate the community's contributions and advocate for the acceptance and recognition of the community.

Our CoP conducted an exit interview when one of our sponsors resigned from the organization. One of the questions we asked was, "What do you see as the ideal sponsor for a CoP for admins?" In response, he describes an ideal sponsor should be invested in the community's success of the practice and take an active role in its development.

Additionally, the ideal sponsor should be knowledgeable about the CoP's topics and be able to provide resources and support when needed.

CREATING A CORE TEAM

A core team of leaders is essential to guide the work and activities of a CoP. Establishing a CoP requires a lot of work to set up and sustain over time. Volunteers, and activities around leading, monitoring and evaluating, create an effective CoP. This is important when selecting candidates to fill key roles.

Essential to the success of any community of practice, this team handles developing and managing the community of practice programs and activities and best practices to meet the CoP's goals. The structure of a CoP may include:

> A **coordinator**, the face of the community of practice, who has the primary responsibility to support members of the core team, guide the development of chapters, and translate the CoP programs within the organization.
>
> **Core Team Members** represent each of the areas across the organization. These representatives lead programs, projects, or initiatives on behalf of your CoP.
>
> **Sponsorship** is beneficial but not necessary. Due to the nature of our work and the content having the potential to be misunderstood within a unionized environment, we opted for a governance
>
> model to ensure support from the organization and the union(s) within it. We have two levels of sponsorship.

The executive sponsor in this structure is who we report to and seek implementation approvals. The CoP level sponsor provides guidance on operational activities. The Core Team structure was set up to provide leadership opportunities for our members by taking on key roles within our structure to support the work undertaken by the CoP. I have included in the appendix, samples of role statements for our working groups, project teams and committees.

FOUNDATIONAL DOCUMENTS

In addition to a formalized structure, there is a need for developing foundational documents to guide the work of the CoP. Earlier, I mentioned having a Charter. A Charter has information on how the community of practice will interact with its members and the organization. A Charter is a document that helps define the role and activities of a CoP in relation to an organization's overarching goals. Finally, a Charter articulates the community's purpose, aims, and scope and can help legitimize the CoP in the organization.

The term "Charter" is more often used in a project-based environment. It is a way to document information required by decision-makers to approve and support the activities of the project as they relate to the specific project.

Studies by the American Productivity and Quality Center (APQC) revealed in 2021, that 91% of CoPs requiring or using a Charter are more effective than those who do not. I recommend developing on as it provides your members with guiding principles of why you exist, what you plan to do, and how you will be able to execute and sustain the work. Our leadership has asked tough questions, like "how are you going to know the CoP is successful?" "How are you going to measure the impact the CoP has had on building capacity?" The Charter helped us answer them and determined what was out of our scope.

Your Charter's purpose statement should be clear, concise, and unambiguous. It should communicate the CoP's mission and goals, as well as the reasons for undertaking the project. Your purpose statement should address the following questions: What are we trying to achieve? Why are we undertaking this project? What are the key principles that will guide our actions?

Writing a charter can be a daunting task, but it doesn't have to be. In this article, we will be discussing the do's and don'ts of writing a community of practice charter. By following these tips, you can be sure that your charter will be clear, concise, and effective.

There are a few things to keep in mind when writing a Community of Practice charter. First, make sure the purpose of the group is clear. What is the group trying to achieve? Who will be involved? What kind of commitment is required from participants? Once you have answered these questions, you can move on to drafting the actual charter.

When it comes time to write the charter, there are a few Dos and Don'ts to keep in mind:

- Do spell out what role each member will play within the community, so everyone knows what their responsibilities are

- Don't forget that collaboration requires give-and-take – make sure all members feel like they have a chance to contribute equally

- Do use simple language that everyone can understand – this isn't an academic exercise, it's about working together towards a common goal

- Don't try to do too much – focus on one or two specific objectives and leave room for flexibility as your community grows and changes over time

It is important to have a clear and concise charter. This document will serve as the guiding principles for the group, so it is essential that all members agree with its content. With that being said, there are some things you should avoid when writing your charter:

- Don't make assumptions about what everyone wants from the group – take the time to consult with potential members beforehand to get an idea of what they would like to see included in the charter.

- Avoid using jargon or technical terms that not everyone will understand – remember that this document needs to be accessible to all members of the community, regardless of their level of expertise.

- Don't forget to consider logistics such as meeting times/frequency and how decisions will be made by the group – these details may seem trivial, but they can actually have a big impact on whether or not people participate in your community of practice

Tips To Writing a Compelling Charter

There are a few key things to keep in mind when writing a community of practice charter. First, it's important to be clear about the purpose and goals of the group. What is this community of practice meant to achieve? Who will benefit from its work? Be as specific as possible here.

Next, consider what kind of structure and governance will best support the community's work. How often will members meet? Who will facilitate discussions and coordinate activities? What decision-making processes will be used? Again, being clear and specific here is crucial.

Finally, think about how you can create buy-in from potential members by making the charter itself compelling. This means crafting an inspiring vision for the group that speaks to its purpose and goals; outlining concrete benefits for participating; and detailing any expectations around commitment or participation (e.g., regular attendance at meetings).

A sample charter template has been included in Appendix 3 for your reference. Be sure to research other sources until you find the one that best meets your needs.

LESSONS LEARNED - BUILDING YOUR TEAM

Our first team was literally hand-picked and made up of individuals interested in trying to build capacity --- buy-in already existed. We prepared two guiding documents for the community, a Charter and a *"Competency Development Framework for Administrative Professionals"*[4]. This document is the foundation of the work undertaken by the community.

With sponsors in place, a presentation to our senior executives seeking support to move forward with this initiative was made. The response for support was overwhelming and now there was no turning back.

---

[4] Framework was adapted from the works of the Government of Newfoundland and Labrador.

Once we presented the idea to our senior leadership, other executives wanted their senior admin to be involved at this level. This became our "core team" and included the executive assistant from each division and a few others who started the work. To ensure all areas were represented, we also invited members so their voices could be shared.

The biggest challenge was engagement. We now had some with buy-in and some who were not quite with us. Their comments included, "I am here because my manager told me I had to be". It had taken nearly three years to gain their buy-in with the core team members of the CoP I mentioned throughout. Engagement and relationship building is key from the onset.

What made this so successful? Focusing on the current needs and how a CoP could support those needs while working in tandem to achieving the organizational goals. It was not difficult for the senior executives to buy in to this proposed work. We were on our way to making a massive change in an organization of more than 100,000 employees across the province. Our executive sponsor once commented, "be careful; good news spreads fast."

Our virtual site was built using a SharePoint platform. The foundational documents created include the Charter, Terms of Reference, and the framework.

We were now ready to execute the community of practice, roll out activities and recognize contributions. Oh boy we thought, we were only ten people; how are we going to bring this to potential members? Let us have a celebration! The timing was right to hold an event in conjunction with Administrative Professionals Day. We had games and prizes and enrolled 34 of a potential 180 members within 24 hours of our launch.

Our site was ready for showcasing, so we created an escape room to display each section. What was unique about this launch was that our core team learned several new skills using existing tools – we never used PowerPoint like this before.

We learned how to use animations, impose characters over backgrounds, and provide hints and clues in the rooms. Our core team learned new skills together. It was so much fun and exhilarating.

Below summarizes the lessons learned during the conception of the CoP:

- Accept that not all people want to be part of something big, significant or something that changes organizational culture.

- Acknowledge engagement is an ongoing activity even with your CoP leaders.

- People are skeptical and not always comfortable moving out of their comfort zone, nor will they see the value of a CoP.

The work then begins in earnest to keep members engaged, providing value and relevant information that meets their needs. The next chapter will discuss engaging members and barriers to engagement experiences.

Engaging Members

"...You have to want to be engaged. There has to be deep-seated desire in your heart and mind to participate, to be involved, and to make a difference. If the desire isn't there, no person or book can plant it within you." -- Tim Clark

The key to a thriving CoP is engaging its members. By getting members involved and invested in the group, they will be more likely to participate and contribute to the CoP. Member involvement strengthens the group and allows individuals to learn from one another and grow their skills. Participation also encourages social connections and relationships within the group, making the CoP more enjoyable and supportive.

To engage members, CoP leaders should focus on creating opportunities for interaction and collaboration, through online forums, social media groups, in-person meetings, or other events. Whatever the format, it is important to provide members with a space to connect and share their knowledge. Additionally, leaders should make sure to encourage new ideas and dissenting opinions. This will keep the group dynamic and help it to continue evolving.

While participation is essential to a CoP, it is also important that members feel like they can contribute in a way that is meaningful to them.

Leaders should consider what each member can offer and how they can utilize their skills in a meaningful way by inviting them to provide their creativity while designing a presentation or delegating a task that draws on their strengths.

This may involve assigning specific roles or tasks, or it could simply mean giving members the freedom to choose how they want to contribute. Ultimately, the goal is to ensure everyone feels like they can add value to the group.

MEMBERSHIP ENGAGEMENT LEVELS

Before I provide some suggestions for engaging members, we need to understand the levels of engagement our members have. A description of the various levels of participation[5] is provided below.

> **Active** – These members work closely with the core team to help shape the definition and direction of the CoP, which includes defining the community's shared vision, purpose, roles, strategies for interaction, marketing, and communications.
>
> **Occasional** – These members participate when specific topics of interest are addressed or when they have something to contribute to the group. They are often the largest group in the community.

---

[5] *SAFe®, Scaled Agile Framework, Communities of Practice,* 2022

Peripheral – These members feel connected to the community of practice but engage on a limited basis. These could be newcomers or those with a more casual interest in the community of practice activities.

Transactional – These members are the least connected to the community of practice. They connect only to access CoP resources or to provide a specific service to the CoP (for example, website support).

It is common for people to move between different levels of participation and commitment over time. CoPs are self-organizing, and their members have the freedom to determine their level of engagement that is different from other working groups, such as project teams, task forces, and committees.

The natural movement of people among communities and levels is healthy. It allows new knowledge and fresh ideas to flow across the organization in ways that are different but complementary to formal information-sharing.

By creating a CoP that is engaging and supportive, leaders can create an environment conducive to learning and growth.

They will make the CoP more effective and beneficial for everyone involved. Engagement needs to occur at every stage and life cycle of the community of practice.

FIVE APPROACHES TO ENGAGEMENT

There are many approaches to engaging your membership. Below are five of the common approaches our CoP found helpful to increase the participation of our members.

Introduce the CoP to the orientation process for new hires. Yes, new hires for the first few weeks will find it overwhelming. The CoP and its resources can help the transition period for new employees.

Invest in marketing and branding opportunities. Our CoP has restrictions on branding criteria based on organizational standards. A branding expert can help develop a familiar look/feel to the CoP-related materials. Recognizable imagery for tools, programs and sites will bolster membership and visibility.

Promotion through events/activities. Seize the moment to share information about the CoP. An elevator speech, for example, is a great opportunity to tell people you meet about your involvement in a CoP and what you are gaining from it.

Promotional resources are designed to support professional development activities. Self-promote your participation, and your desire to take part in CoP activities. Your annual review process is a great place to start.

Seek out opportunities to present at meetings outside your division. Sharing information spreads faster when people see the good things that are happening. Be proud to share these at every moment that comes your way.

The Benefits of Engagement

There are four phases during the engagement process. You will encounter resistance, resignation, acceptance, and embracing as your CoP evolves. Keeping members engaged should be an ongoing focus of the CoP leadership.

In my experience, one of the best ways to achieve buy-in is to share the benefits associated with the program or change, "What's in it for me?". Lisa Nelson, summed it up clearly in her article, *"What are the Benefits of a Community of Practice (CoP)"* which I am sharing with you below:

Increased Collaboration: connecting people and creating a path for people to interact, pool resources, and work together. Relationships with other areas have been our greatest win...people are talking to one another.

Exchange of Information and Ideas: A CoP provides the context for people to communicate and share information and ideas. The sharing of experiences had by its members is priceless and so beneficial, bringing truth to the cliché, "learn from your mistakes".

Innovate and create new ideas/knowledge: Individually, you may feel you are not an innovator or creative, but the collectiveness of a CoP brings unlimited opportunities.

Professional Development: Finding the right mix of learning groups and educational workshops helps professional development and increase productivity and performance.

Rapid Problem-Solving: With a CoPs makeup of ability, problem-solving can be fast and results oriented. In addition, individuals are enhancing their critical thinking skills.

An Environment of Trust: Another benefit of a CoP is that it provides a context for people to communicate and share information and knowledge, which helps to build relationships and create a sense of community within the group. In addition, it can help people to learn from each other and to collaborate more effectively.

Obstacles to Engagement

> *"Effective professional learning must be consistent, targeted, and job embedded. Otherwise, it is a hope, not a practice." -- Allison Rodman*

Any effort to change the environment or add new programs will hinder success. In this section, I will share the barriers we faced with the Achieving More Together community of practice.

No Change is Necessary

The first impediment is the belief that nothing needs to change. People are often comfortable with the status quo or do not see how the proposed change will benefit them.

For our CoP, some members were reluctant to try new ways of doing things because they saw no need to fix what was working. It was only after we showed them how the proposed changes could make their work easier. They then were willing to give it a try. Let us look at other barriers.

Lack of Capacity

If you have established communities of practice, bringing new skills into an organization becomes easier. With varying skills, abilities and the expectation placed on admins, building capacity across the organization is critical.

When a CoP consists of people who share a particular role, it can help the organization by being responsible for hiring staff for that role and developing new employees once they arrive. Having a CoP in place is attractive to potential hires. Knowing that you are joining a ready-made support network is an additional bonus in a new job.

If the community of practice has an identity and a set of values, those values can help to identify who is a good fit for the role. If the community of practice can articulate skills gaps and development needs, they can look for someone with the skills to fill those gaps. The community can then support the new hires once they arrive.

The community of practice needs to collectively agree on the skills required for the role. They then used this set of skills to refine the existing job description, help members set objectives and create career paths for that role, which meant that a community of practice members agreed on what good professional development looked like for a specific role.

A capacity model is a visual or textual representation of an organization's different capacities and the relationships between them. The community recognized the ability to build capacity through shared competencies, skills, orientation, and knowledge.

The diagram on the below identifies a community of practice the sharing of knowledge and training, competencies are developed to achieve excellence in the administrative professional's field. do only include skills and knowledge in a particular area, but it also includes individual attitudes that influence how individuals think, feel, and behave.

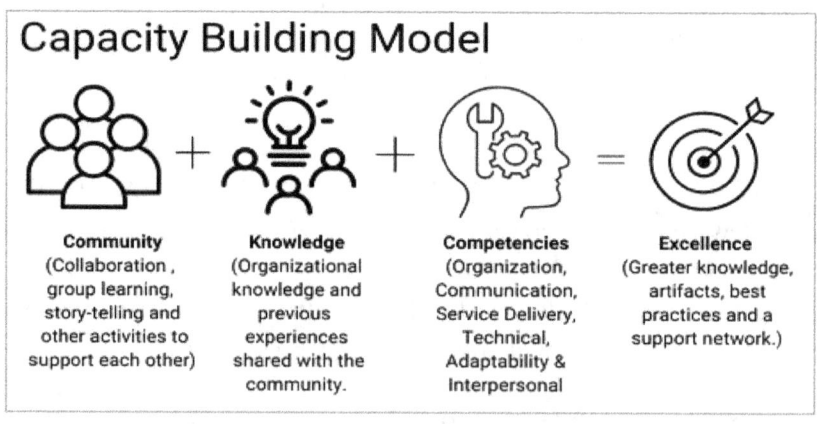

Source: *Capacity Building Model, Carol Walsh, 2022*

These behaviours need to align with organizational values as well. The diagram above symbolizes a capacity model that achieves excellence.

Using a capacity model helps the organization identify its different capacities and the relationships between them, which allows the organization to understand better how it can improve its ability to achieve its goals.

Additionally, organizing events and planning activities that would interest the group is another way to engage leadership.

It is important to remember that every group is different and what works for one may not work for another.

Some ways to engage members and promote CoP activities include providing support, learning resources, holding events, and facilitating discussions which help members learn and improve their skills. Hosting events helps generate interest and gets members involved. Facilitating debate allows for the exchange of ideas and helps build relationships. All these together create a community that is engaged and supportive of each other.

It is vital to have a mix of skill-building activities to engage members from across the program. Some examples of activities are webinars, conferences, discussion forums, training sessions, and networking events, which will meet the needs of the group.

For example, I might use a webinar to introduce new members to the CoP, and a conference could be used to showcase the work of the program.

Discussion forums are a great way to get members talking and exchanging ideas, while training sessions can help learn new skills. Networking events are a great way to build relationships and promote the CoP. There is no one-size-fits-all solution, so it is important to experiment and see what works best for your community. By engaging leadership and members, you can create a supportive and thriving community that contributes to the success of the CoP.

Lack of Participation

With any CoP, barriers are faced along the road to success. Engagement with a virtual CoP was my biggest challenge. I could see icon images of the participants – unable to gauge their level of interest or participation through their body language. Jenny Smith's and Teresa A. Sherman's article, "*Virtual Communities of Practice: 9 Tips to Engage Participation*", outlines tips for engagement in hosting an online meeting.

> The silence is deafening, and I could not understand why no one was contributing. Administrative professionals are often called upon to complete tasks, sometimes while they are in meetings. We try to be the best multitaskers in the organization. A virtual setting is easy for the membership to get off track and be interrupted by other teammates. Smith and Sherman suggest people are not talking or contributing because:
>
> There may be a **misunderstanding** about what the expectations of the CoP are. For example, is it a listen-and-learn environment, or a participatory conversation?
>
> They may feel **discomfort** because the environment feels formal. Participants may feel the event is more like a public engagement, not a conversation with peers. If the session allows, consider using icebreakers. They may help with gauging the temperature of the room.

There may be a **perceived hierarchy**. A CoP consists of peers; there should be no hierarchy. Sharing sometimes makes people feel vulnerable as well, creating an uncomfortable environment.

The participants may be **multitasking** and not present which may directly result from workload issues and can be very disruptive to a group. Encourage your membership to be actively taking part.

There may be some **skepticism**. For some people, talking and not doing it make it challenging to buy in. Possibly they have not seen the benefits on a personal level or reinforcement, which reinforces the tangible benefits. Individuals need satisfaction and personal rewards.

Lack of Support from Leaders

Active support from leaders is essential for engaged members. Leaders can provide resources, opportunities, and recognition that members need to stay involved.

They also play a role in addressing engagement problems. If members are having trouble getting involved, leaders can help identify the problem and find a solution. Leaders can also provide support to members who are struggling to stay engaged.

Competing Organizational Priorities

Limitations to engagement we encountered is competing priorities within the organization. Workload issues and lack of support are often reasons members become disengaged. Sometimes trying to control the actions of admins leads to barriers. Here is an example of what occurred in the CoP.

Early in the development of our CoP, an individual (a core team member) demanded the removal of four individuals from our CoP. She was rather adamant that I do this. Since we have voluntary membership, I needed to find out why.

She responded, "we have our training program at our location; they do not need the CoP. I want to control the information they receive." After I got over the initial shock, I chose not to remove the individuals. They showed a desire to participate -- it was not her decision to make.

We continued to engage with them and provide them with information about our CoP, and they eventually became engaged members.

Perceptions

When members perceive that their participation in the CoP will not be valued or appreciated can create a roadblock.

We have tried to address this by being clear about the expectations for participation and highlighting how each member's contributions are valuable to the group. We also make a point of thanking members for their participation, both publicly and privately.

Through feedback, it was revealed that a department decided their classification was not entitled to our resources…". This situation if not addressed would have had an impact on human resources and the union. Situations like these do not support the engagement of members. All administrative professionals are included in the work and offerings of the CoP.

Keeping current members engaged requires time and commitment from the CoP leaders. Securing active support from the organizational leaders lends credibility to the program and conveys how vital the CoP is to the organization. Obtaining their consent is crucial if the activities are taking place during work time.

The bottom line is that engagement of leaders is critical to reducing organizational priority barriers and promoting flexibility for our members.

Distance Between Members

Distance between members of a CoP could be limiting to some. Virtual CoPs create opportunities for flexibility. Using the right tools enables collaboration, bringing members closer.

Although there are few studies on virtual CoPs, the evidence suggests they have the same value as in-person. The virtual CoP enables collaboration and information sharing.

Success is not related to whether you are virtual or in-person; success comes through the CoPs leadership, champions, and networks as people. Regardless of the setting, the opportunity for building relations comes from its members. Relationships need time to grow and develop. As well as the need for strong leadership and champions to be successful.

Here are some tips for ongoing engagement:

- Schedule regular meetings and communications such as newsletters, blogs, discussions, and announcements.
- Summarize events and highlight in your newsletter.
- Find your champions and ask them to help.
- Ask for webcams to be turned on for better engagement; it can turn out to be fun.
- Create themes for your meetings to bring out your member's creativity.
- Mix up the formats by using an icebreaker or conducting a fun poll, for example.

Keeping the Momentum

"The rhythm of daily action aligned with your goals creates the momentum that separates dreamers from super-achievers." — Darren Hardy

When it comes to creating and sustaining a community of practice, it is important to remember that momentum is key. If you can create a sense of excitement and enthusiasm among your members, they will be more likely to stick around and participate. This section will discuss the different stages of a community of practice's life cycle, as well as some tips for maintaining momentum.

A community of practice goes through different stages as it progresses. Here we will discuss the three main stages: formation, maturation, and decline. Each stage has its own unique challenges, which must be addressed to keep the community moving forward. Let us take a closer look!

The **formation stage** is when the community is just getting started. At this point, it is important to focus on recruitment and building relationships. You will also need to establish some guidelines and rules for participation. This is the time to get people excited about what the community has to offer.

The **maturation stage** is when the community has been established and is starting to grow. At this point, you will need to focus on keeping things organized and running smoothly. You will also need to continue recruiting new members and keeping existing members engaged. This is the time to start thinking about sustainability.

The **decline stage** is when the community starts to dwindle. At this point, you will need to focus on re-engagement. You will also need to think about ways to attract new members and keep existing members involved. This is the time to start thinking about how to revitalize the community. Some recommendations:

1. Keep things organized and running smoothly during the maturation stage. This will help keep the community moving forward.

2. Continue recruiting new members and keeping existing members engaged during the maturation stage. This will help ensure the community's growth.

3. Focus on re-engaging members during the decline stage. This will help prevent the community from dwindling away.

4. Think about ways to attract new members and keep existing members involved during the decline stage. This will help revitalize the community.

If you keep these tips in mind, you will be well on your way to creating and sustaining a successful community of practice.

Refreshing the CoP

When you find other activities that do not seem to be keeping the momentum going, it may be time to reimagine the CoP. I would like to spend a little time on this topic because it seemed to be the most critical in my experience. Throughout the existence of your CoP, there will be a need to step back and refresh. Here are a few suggestions:

- Redefine membership criteria to address engagement challenges.
- Change formats, times, and topics of shifting timing issues.
- Revisit the purpose and initiatives of the CoP.

When your CoP reaches a stage where it needs a refresh, there are a few things you can do to shake things up. Try seeking input from your membership, involving members in presenting best-practice work, adding new facilitation methods, or holding general information sessions. Ensure the changes you make will be helpful and improve the functioning of your CoP.

Some other ideas that come to mind are:

Host a special event – inviting all current and past members to come together for a networking event, sharing best practices, and brainstorming new ideas.

Organize a group volunteer project – working together to complete a community service project can help bring CoP members together and foster a sense of teamwork.

Create an online space – if your CoP does not already have an online presence, creating a website, or social media group can help members stay connected and allow for more flexible participation.

Implement new facilitation methods – trying new ways of running meetings and discussions can help breathe new life into the CoP and make it more engaging for members.

Launch a new program or information session – giving members a chance to ask questions and learn more about the CoP can help increase understanding and buy-in. As a general information session, we implemented a monthly "Community Coffee Chat", a 30-minute discussion on a relevant article published for our profession. Another piece we added was "Techy Tips Tuesdays" where we offered drop-in sessions on different technical applications related to our roles.

These are just a few ideas to get you started --- endless possibilities exist! The important thing is to involve your members in the refresh process and make sure that any changes you make will improve the functioning of your CoP.

Despite the challenges the COVID-19 pandemic brought to all of us, the CoP survived and maintained a positive level of engagement from its members, including many of whom were redeployed to support the response.

SCALING AND ENGAGING NEW MEMBERS

In addition to reimagining a CoP, one of the best ways to ensure continued success is to scale and engage new members. This can be a challenge, but the benefits are numerous.

For one, it helps to ensure that the community is always growing and evolving. New members bring new perspectives and ideas, which can keep the community fresh and relevant. Additionally, engaged members are more likely to be active participants, which can lead to a more vibrant and productive community.

Of course, scaling and engaging new members is not always easy. It takes effort and planning to identify and reach potential new members. But the rewards are well worth it. A successful community of practice can be a powerful tool for promoting collaboration and knowledge sharing.

> Scaling and engaging new members in a CoP can have many benefits. First, it helps to ensure that the collective knowledge within the group is constantly evolving and growing. Second, it keeps the group dynamic and vibrant, which can lead to more creative solutions to problems. Finally, scaling and engaging new members also allows for fresh perspectives on old issues – something that is essential for any organization or business. By scaling your community of practice, you can reach more people and have a greater impact. Here are five benefits of scaling:

Create New Networks - You can engage more members of the community. When you scale, you can tap into new networks of potential members who may not be aware of your community otherwise. This allows you to grow the size of your engaged member base, which leads to a larger collective knowledge pool that everyone can benefit from.

Deepen Relationships - As your community scales, so does the interaction between members. Deeper relationships form as bonds are strengthened through shared experiences and common goals - this increased level of connection results in improved collaboration and creativity within the group as a whole.

Diverse Perspectives - When you scale up your membership, you also bring in different perspectives from various backgrounds and walks of life. This diversity can make for richer discussions, problem-solving sessions, and overall idea generation within the group.

Find New Skill Sets - As your CoP grows, so too does the collective skill set represented therein; this can be an invaluable resource when tackling tough challenges or working on complex projects since there's likely someone in the group with expertise in whatever area you need assistance with.

Share Fresh Ideas - New blood always brings with it new energy and excitement which can translate into renewed vigor for taking on old problems in creative ways of approaching tasks from unique angles.

Engaging new members is not always easy, but there are some things that communities of practice can do to encourage it. For example, they can make sure that their website or online presence is up-to-date and inviting and offer incentives for people to join up. There may also be times when existing members need to take a step back so that new voices can be heard - but overall, engaging newcomers should be seen as a positive process that will benefit everyone involved. Scaling and engaging can help the CoP achieve its goals by ensuring everyone is on the same page when it comes to goals, objectives, and mission.

Additionally, this will also help build trust within the group as well as foster a sense of belonging. Finally, by regularly communicating with members and getting their feedback, you can make sure that your community of practice is always moving forward in the right direction.

Engaging new members keep the CoP fresh and relevant. New members bring new perspectives and ideas, which can lead to new insights and discoveries. Employing Chapter Sites can help with scaling. Our CoP showed signs of being stale, it was time to invite members from outside of our division.

The best way to do that was through a chapter. Recognizing other divisions have a different focus on their work, the chapters were designed to meet the specialized needs, interests, or work requirements that differ from the core CoP. You still have access to resources of the overarching community, but you also have your own space to focus on those specific needs. Also, as a chapter, you have expanded your access to other experts in your field gaining insight and perspective from other members. This type of knowledge sharing is invaluable and can help you develop new skills and techniques.

These platforms offer a unique opportunity to network with other professionals and build relationships. You can also use them to collaborate on projects, share best practices, and get feedback on your work.

If you are looking to stay up to date on the latest industry news, chapter sites and communities of practice are also great resources. You can use them to learn about new products, services, and trends. You can also learn about upcoming events, conferences, and workshops.

Finally, chapter sites and communities of practice can also help you achieve your professional development goals. Whether you are looking to advance in your career or transition into a new field, these platforms can give you the resources and support you need to succeed.

When is it time?

As with any program or initiative there is a life cycle. At some point in time the CoP will be no longer effective. There are many signals that time is approaching. How do you know when it is time to shut it down? This section will provide you some signals and opportunities to save the CoP.

It is important to recognize changes in member behaviour throughout the life cycle of a CoP. For example, we noticed a decline in attendance at our monthly training sessions.

There could be many reasons for this, such as:

Timing – does this time conflict with other responsibilities for our members.

Topics – not meeting the needs of our members.

Engagement – members lose interest in the CoP and its activities. Milestones were reached and no new initiatives were identified.

Shifting organizational priorities.

When a CoP has run its course, you will see some members letting go while others want to engage and continue. Leadership has a role to play in keeping the momentum moving.

Here are some strategies that can be employed to help with transitioning, especially for the dedicated leaders of the CoP:

- Helping them let go can be difficult, but it is important to encourage your members to recognize their achievements and explore new opportunities. Seeking out new relationships and carrying on is vital to the community's success.

- Celebrating and communicating successes is also essential and wrapping up with a celebration can help members feel recognized for their valuable work.

- Telling stories is a great way to preserve the knowledge of the community, and artifacts can be important in maintaining relationships after the community has ended.

- Planning periodic reunions can also help keep members connected.

Maintaining the momentum of a CoP is important for ensuring its success. Leaders can help by encouraging members to explore new opportunities and maintain relationships with each other. Celebrating successes and telling stories are also great ways to keep the community connected.

Getting Feedback

"I think it's very important to have a feedback loop, where you're constantly thinking about what you've done and how you could be doing it better."
-- Elon Musk

Working within a community of practice can be extremely beneficial for administrative assistants looking to improve their skills and knowledge. However, in order for a community of practice to be truly effective, it is important to ensure that feedback is incorporated. Feedback questions are an excellent way to facilitate this process.

When used correctly, feedback questions can help to improve the overall quality of the community of practice by ensuring that members are constantly learning and growing Additionally, feedback questions can help to identify areas where the community of practice can improve.

In this chapter, we will be discussing how to use feedback questions to improve your community of practice. We will be exploring the different types of feedback questions, as well as how to effectively incorporate them into the community of practice.

Establishing a Feedback Question Process

Are you looking to improve your community of practice? If so, feedback questions can be a great way to do this. By asking for feedback from members of your community on a regular basis, you can get valuable insights into what is working well and what could be improved. To follow are some considerations to establishing a process to obtain feedback:

> **Set some ground rules** - decide how often you will ask for feedback (weekly, monthly, etc.), who will answer the questions (all members, just leaders, etc.), and how the answers will be used (anonymous or not).
>
> **Choose the right platform** - there are many different platforms that you can use to collect feedback from your community. Find one that will work best for your needs.
>
> **Ask away!** - Now it's time to start asking those feedback questions. Be sure to vary them up so that all areas of your community are covered.

By following these steps, you can establish a strong feedback question process that will help you continuously improve your community of practice.

Determining What Type of Feedback Questions to Use

When it comes to feedback, one size does not necessarily fit all. The type of feedback questions you use should be based on the specific needs and goals of your community of practice. Here are a few things to keep in mind when determining which feedback questions will work best for your group:

> **What is the purpose of the feedback?** Is it meant to assess progress, identify areas needing improvement, or simply generate discussion? Depending on the purpose, different types of questions may be more appropriate.
>
> **Who will be answering the questions?** Will it just be members of the community of practice, or will outsiders also be involved? If outside perspectives are needed, open-ended questions may work better than closed-ended ones.
>
> **How much time do you have** for collecting and analyzing responses? If time is limited, shorter surveys with fewer question types may be preferable.

Asking the Right People, the Right Questions

One of the most important things you can do to improve your community of practice is to ask for feedback. But it's not enough to just ask anyone for their opinion - you need to make sure you're asking the right people the right questions.

Who should you be asking? Look for people who are actively involved in your community and who have a variety of perspectives. You want a mix of opinions, so don't just go to your friends or colleagues - reach out beyond your immediate circle. And what kind of questions should you be asking? Avoid yes/no questions or leading questions that could bias responses. Instead, focus on open-ended questions that will give insights into what works well and what needs improvement. For example: "What did you think about our last event?" or "How can we make our website more user-friendly?" By gathering this type of feedback, you'll be able to identify areas where changes need to be made - and ultimately create a stronger community as a result."

Using Feedback to Improve Your Community of Practice

When it comes to feedback, don't be afraid to ask for it! If you want to improve your community of practice, seek out feedback from others. This can be done in a number of ways, such as conducting surveys or interviews with members.

Not only will this help you identify areas that need improvement, but it will also show members that you value their input and are committed to making the community the best it can be.

Of course, not all feedback is created equal. In order to get useful information that will actually help improve your community, make sure to craft thoughtful questions that solicit specific responses. For example, rather than simply asking "What do you think of our group?" try something

Like "What topics would you like discussed at our next meeting?" or "What events or activities would interest you in attending?" By taking the time to create quality questions, you'll ensure that the feedback received is valuable and actionable.

Remember that Feedback should be ongoing – not just a one-time thing! Once you have collected initial data from your survey or interview process described above), continue seeking out regular input from members on an ongoing basis; this could be done through informal conversations or more formalized mechanisms such as focus groups.

Getting the Most Out of Feedback Questions

One way to get the most out of feedback questions is to avoid yes/no or either/or responses. When possible, ask open-ended questions that encourage elaboration and discussion.

For example, instead of asking "Did you like the training?" try something like "What did you think of the training?" This allows people to share their thoughts and feelings more fully, providing valuable insights into what worked well and what could be improved.

Another tip for getting the most out of feedback questions is to make sure they are relevant to your community of practice. Ask about topics that everyone can relate to and that will generate useful information for improving future events or activities.

For example, rather than asking general questions about a recent conference, focus on specific aspects such as breakout sessions, keynote speakers, networking opportunities, etc. By zeroing in on specific areas, you'll gather more targeted feedback that can be put to good use right away.

After collecting feedback from your community members via surveys or other means), take some time to review the results carefully and develop a plan for how you'll act on the suggestions received. Remember the value you will gain when you follow up after the results have been provided. Let people know what changes have been made based on their input - this shows that their voices are being heard loud and clear!

Feedback questions are a great place to start if you're looking to improve your community of practice.

By asking questions and actively listening to the answers, you can get a better understanding of what's working well and what could be improved. Plus, you can use feedback to identify any gaps in your community's knowledge or skills.

Asking feedback questions can be daunting, but it doesn't have to be. Just start with a few simple questions and go from there. And remember, feedback is a two-way street. So be sure to give as well as receive. With a little effort, you can create a thriving community of practice that everyone can benefit from.

Monitoring Success

"A useful metric is both accurate (in that it measures what it says it measures) and aligns with your goals. Don't measure anything unless the data helps you make better decisions or change your actions."
-- Seth Godin

I mentioned previously some principles that lead to the success of a CoP. Other factors contributing to success include:

Active participation. CoPs rely on their members' active involvement, which includes sharing information and ideas and engaging in discussion and debate.

Open communication. Members need to feel comfortable communicating with each other, both online and offline and includes both sharing information and ideas and engaging in discussion and debate.

Trust and respect. For a CoP to be successful, the members need to trust and respect each other. This trust and respect should be based on mutual interests and goals, and not on hierarchy or authority.

Support from leadership. A CoP is more likely to be successful if it has the support of leadership. This could include financial support, but also things like allowing members to use work time to participate in the CoP.

CoPs can be a great way for members to learn from each other and improve their skills. If you are thinking of starting a CoP, or are already a member of one, keep these success factors in mind.

Some reasons why CoPs may be unsuccessful could be a lack of a core group/committee or low levels of one-to-one interaction between members. The CoP may have been rigid in terms of their competencies or do not have a sense of identification with the community. They cannot tangibly demonstrate their practices.

You will recall for a CoP to be effective; members must interact regularly. This interaction can take many forms, such as discussions, sharing information and resources, joint problem-solving, and peer learning. However, research has shown that communities of practice often fail to live up to their potential due to several factors.

One of the main reasons why communities of practice fail is because they lack a core group or committee. Without a central group to provide guidance and direction, CoPs can quickly become disorganized and ineffective, additionally, challenging to make decisions or keep track of progress without a designated leader.

Another reason why communities of practice fail is because of the low level of interaction between members. If members do not interact with each other regularly, they will quickly lose touch with what is happening in the group and will be less likely to contribute to its success. Additionally, if there is no interaction between members, it can be challenging to build trust and rapport.

Finally, communities of practice can also fail due to the rigidity of their competencies. If a CoP is too rigid in its structure and goals, it will be difficult for members to adapt and change as the needs of the group evolve. As well, if a community is too focused on one specific area, it may miss opportunities to learn from other groups or members.

When a CoP fails, there are usually three things that need to happen to remedy the situation. First, the community members need to identify the reason for the failure. Second, they need to develop a plan to address the issue. Third, they need to put the plan into action and see if it works. If it does not, they need to return to the drawing board and try again.

Identifying the reason for the failure is the first step in fixing a failing CoP. Without knowing the cause of the problem, it will not be easy to develop an effective plan to address it. There are many different reasons why a CoP might fail, so it is important to take the time to figure out what the specific problem is.

When you suspect the CoP has lost interest or no longer meets its purpose, the next step is developing a tailored plan to address the issue. For example, suppose the problem is that members are not engaging with the community.

In that case, the plan might involve developing new outreach methods or creating more opportunities for members to interact with each other. If the problem is that the community is not effective at solving problems, the plan might involve developing better ways to share knowledge or improving communication between members.

When you reach the need to develop a "recovery plan" it is time for the community members to work together to implement it. If the plan is successful, it should result in rejuvenating the community's performance.

A failing CoP can be a frustrating experience, but it is important to remember that all communities go through ups and downs. By taking the time to identify the problem and develop a plan to address it and break the cycle so the community can get back on track and become successful once again.

As a member you have a part to play. The success of a CoP also depends on you. Being a part of a CoP is important for anyone looking to make an impact in their field. It is essential to get involved and take on leadership roles, serve as a resource, be active in discussions and activities, and build relationships with others in the group.

This will help you share your knowledge and expertise with others, strengthening the community. You play a vital role in the success of any organization. It is essential to ensure your voice is heard. Create opportunities to provide the biggest impact in your CoP. Below are some ways you can make an impactful contribution:

- Taking on leadership roles.

- Serving as a resource, sharing your knowledge and expertise with others in the group.

- Participating actively in discussions and activities, offering your insights and perspectives to help move the community forward.

- Building relationships with community members. Get to know people and what they are working on so you can better collaborate and support each other.

- Sharing your knowledge. Being open to sharing information, resources, and ideas with others in the group.

Belonging to a CoP can offer several benefits, including access to expertise and knowledge, networking opportunities, and moral support. Communities of practice can provide a sense of identity and shared purpose, making it easier to overcome challenges and achieve goals.

Participation in a CoP can also help individuals learn new skills and knowledge and develop new ways of thinking about and approaching problems.

Monitoring and Evaluating

One of the most important things to do when monitoring a CoP is to ensure that everyone in the CoP has the same understanding of what the CoP is and what it is trying to achieve. This can be done through regular meetings or other communication methods, such as online forums or chat rooms. To ensure that the CoP remains healthy and cohesive, it is also important to monitor the level of activity and participation by tracking the number of posts or comments made or by measuring the time members spend interacting with each other.

Another critical aspect of monitoring a CoP is to keep an eye out for signs of trouble including members who seem to be disengaged or uninterested in the CoP, or who are constantly arguing with other members. If these signs are spotted, it is important to take action to try and address the issue before it causes severe damage to the CoP.

Finally, monitoring the CoP for changes that could affect its future is also essential and includes changes in the membership, the goals of the CoP, and operation. By keeping an eye on these changes, you can help to ensure that the CoP remains relevant and practical.

Why Measure Performance?

There are a few key reasons why measuring the performance of a CoP can be important.

Help Identify Areas for Improvement: Measuring performance can help to identify areas where the CoP could be improved, whether in terms of the amount or quality of collaboration, the level of expertise among its members, or how well it is meeting its goals.

Builds Trust and Legitimacy: Measuring performance helps to build trust and legitimacy for the CoP among its members and other stakeholders.

Assess Level of Collaboration/Interaction: One way to measure the performance of a CoP is to assess the level of collaboration and interaction among its members through surveys or interviews with CoP members, as well as by observing interactions between members.

Test and Evaluate Members' Knowledge and Level of Expertise: Another performance level of measurement is to test and evaluate members' knowledge by asking questions to determine their level of expertise.

Assessing How Well the CoP is Meeting Their Goals: Additionally, performance can be measured by assessing how well the CoP meets its goals through surveys or interviews with members and by observing CoP activities.

Performance Indicators

In order for the CoP to be effective, it is important to measure its performance in order to identify areas needing improvement. There are three key performance indicators (KPI) for a community of practice: quality, quantity, and engagement.

- **Quality:** This can be measured by looking at how well members are able to achieve their goals. Are they able to find answers to their questions? Do they feel like they are part of a supportive network?

- **Quantity**: This measures how many people are actively participating in the community. A high number indicates that the community is doing a good job of attracting new members and keeping them engaged.

- **Engagement:** How active and involved members are in the community are measured by this indicator group.

There are several key performance indicators (KPI) that can be used to measure the performance of a CoP:

- **Membership:** Number of members for example. This metric measures the size of the community and can give insight into its growth potential. For example: number of new requests; number of new members, etc.

- **Levels of engagement**: This metric looks at how active members are within the community and whether they are participating in discussions, sharing resources, etc. Adoption and Participation could also be captured in this category. Some examples would be number of participants and educational session, number online activities, number of downloads, number of visits to the site.

- **Quality of content:** This metric assesses the usefulness and relevance of the information being shared within the community. Some KPIs here could include documents are current and relevant, best practices and lessons learned; problem solving resources, etc.

- **Improving The Performance:** Key indicators in this category could include value statements and measure the value of the resources from the CoP to its members.

A well-functioning community of practice can be a valuable asset to an organization, providing a source of knowledge and expertise that can be used to improve performance.

There are a number of key performance indicators that can be used to measure the performance of a community of practice. These include the number of members, the level of activity, the quality of the discussions, the number of new ideas generated, and the number of problems solved.

Evaluating Progress

The evaluation of the progress of a CoP using a results framework can be very beneficial in determining the efficacy of the community's work. A results framework can help to identify specific goals that the community has set for itself and track whether these goals are being met.

Additionally, a results framework can help assess the impact of the community of practice's work on its members and the organization.

There are a few different ways to set up a results framework for a CoP. One approach is using a specific set of metrics or indicators to measure progress. These metrics can be quantitative, such as the number of new members joining the community each month.

Metrics may be qualitative, such as the level of satisfaction members report with the community of practice's work.

Another approach is to use a more general results framework, which can adapt to fit the needs of any given community of practice. This framework might include elements such as a mission statement, goals, and objectives. Once these elements have been determined, the community can then begin to track its progress against them.

The approach used is essential to ensure that the designed framework results are accessible and understandable by all community members, which requires reviewing on a regular basis to ensure relevance and usefulness. A results framework is a valuable tool for communities of practice, helping them to track their progress and assess their impact.

By using a results framework, a community of practices can ensure that they stay on track and achieve their goals.

Also, a results framework can help to identify areas where the community of practice needs to improve and provide guidance on how to make those improvements.

Using an Evaluation Framework

With many tools one can use to evaluate their programs you may need to do your research but test the methodology.

We initially attempted our planning and evaluation process using a logic model[6]. We found it was difficult for us to wrap our heads around the theory of the logic model.

After several months of work, we were introduced to a results framework created by TolaData's. This tool's concept focuses on input, activity, output, outcome, and impact. The framework system tracks and manages organizational activities to help generate better output which is the result. The outcome is the effect of an output on a specific target population.

---

[6] Logic Model–A Planning and Evaluation Tool (publichealthontario.ca) is another tool used to plan and evaluation program.

The impact is an organization's overall positive or negative effect on its environment. To effectively manage the outcomes of its activities, an organization must clearly understand the results framework.

The results framework provides a structure for tracking and measuring the consequences of an organization's activities.

It is important to note that the results framework is not a one-size-fits-all solution; it must tailor it to the organization's specific needs.

Not only did our core team find this tool easy to use and interpret we opted to use it instead of the logic model. We found the results framework is a powerful tool for managing outcomes, but it is important to remember that it is not a solution. We learned there are limitations that must be considered when using the results framework.

First, one can only use the framework to track and measure the outcomes of an organization's activities; it cannot improve those outcomes directly. Second, the results framework is only as effective as the data used to populate it. For the results framework to be helpful, accurate and up-to-date data must be collected and entered the system. Third, the results framework is only one piece of the puzzle; it must be used with other tools and processes to manage outcomes effectively.

Despite its limitations, the results framework is valuable for managing outcomes. It can help organizations track and measure progress, identify areas of improvement, and make data-informed decisions. When used correctly, the results framework can be a powerful tool for improving the outcomes of an organization's activities. This process requires dedicated time to complete. If you are reporting to your sponsors, this tool becomes a reporting tool for updating sponsors and the core team, who can use the plan for agendas and meeting updates.

We have implemented a tool using our SharePoint site that allows the various committee leads to update their information and speak to challenges and outcomes during regular meetings. A snapshot of our frameworks and monitoring tool is included in the appendices for your awareness.

Conclusion

> *"Through practice, gently and gradually we can collect ourselves and learn how to be more fully with what we do."* -- Jack Kornfield

A CoP is described as a group of people who come together to share knowledge and expertise to improve their collective ability to solve problems and create value for their discipline and their organization. CoPs can be found in all sorts of organizations, from businesses and nonprofits to schools and government agencies. The benefits of creating and participating in a CoP are vast. To recall some of the benefits of participating in a CoP include:

- Increased knowledge and expertise
- Improved decision-making
- Enhanced creativity
- Greater job satisfaction
- Improved organizational performance

A CoP can be a great asset to any organization, but it is essential to ensure that it aligns with your organization's goals and objectives.

Bringing people together to share knowledge and expertise can help everyone involved become more of an expert in their field and make better decisions.

If you are interested in creating a CoP within your organization, use the tips above to get started.

There are a few key factors that are necessary for a CoP to be successful the members:

- must have a shared domain of interest, expertise, or concern, giving them a common bond and something to bring focus to their discussions.
- must be willing to share their knowledge and expertise including both giving and receiving feedback.
- should feel a sense of community, including trust, mutual respect, and a shared commitment to the group's success.
- should have a platform or forum for members to interact with each other.

Measuring the performance of employees is an integral part of any organization. It allows managers to see how well their team is doing and identify areas where improvement is needed.

As with anything, there are pros and cons to starting a CoP. On the plus side, a CoP can bring people together and help others involved become more of an expert in their field. Additionally, a CoP can help make better decisions by providing a forum for discussion and debate.

On the downside, starting a CoP can be time-consuming and, in some cases, expensive. Additionally, it is important to make sure that the members of a CoP are willing to share their knowledge with others. If not, a CoP may not be the right fit for your organization.

My advice would be to do your research to test your organization's readiness for a learning and development focused CoP for administrative professionals. You do not necessarily need permission to form one, but if you choose to conduct activities during work time, I strongly advise gaining leadership sponsorship and support. Be ready to commit the time and effort.

If you are interested in creating a CoP within your organization, I reiterate the following tips:

- Define the scope of the CoP.
- Identify potential members.
- Create a platform for interaction.
- Encourage sharing.
- Celebrate successes.

Creating a CoP can be a great way to encourage knowledge sharing and collaboration within your organization. Following the steps above, you can start building a successful CoP. It can be helpful to showcase the work of a CoP to encourage other group learning activities, like hosting a conference.

I received a comment from a former Executive Sponsor that was my personal reward for creating a successful community of practice was that we embodied the *"self-generative community of leaders"*.

I hope this book will inspire you to create or join a community of practice.

My belief is that if you build capacity, you build excellence!

APPENDICES

1. Sample of Competency Models

2. Sample Charter Template

3. Checklist to Evaluate Communities of Practice.

4. Sample Framework Results

5. Sample Results Framework Tracking Tool

Appendix 1 - Samples of Competency Models

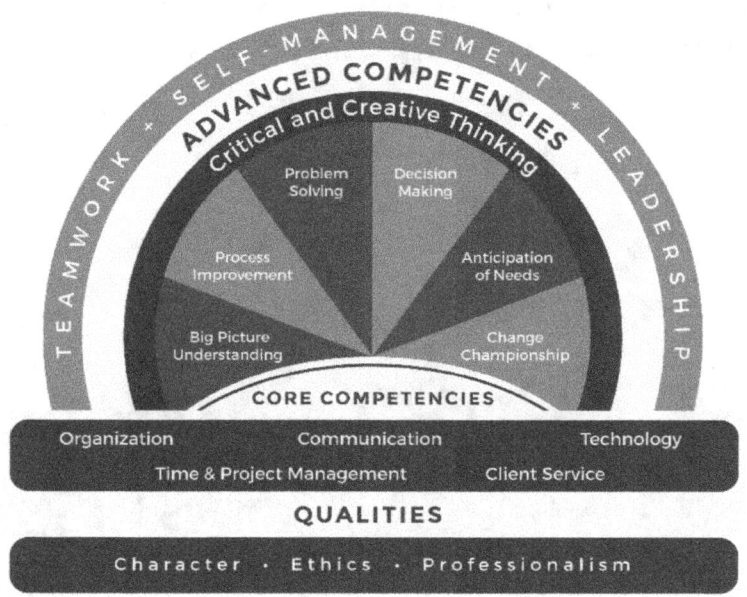

This illustration is shared here with permission from the author. The ELEVATE Admins™ Competency Model is fully owned by Chrissy Scivicque of CCS Ventures, LLC. It cannot be used, copied, printed, or distributed in part or in full without express permission of the author. To learn more, visit
www.ElevateAdmins.com

Star-Performing Administrative Professional Competency Model

This rich combination of attitude, skill, teamwork and strategy leads to performance excellence and career success.

© Copyright Office Dynamics International 2022. All rights reserved. • OfficeDynamics.com • 800-STAR-139

Pillars of Excellence

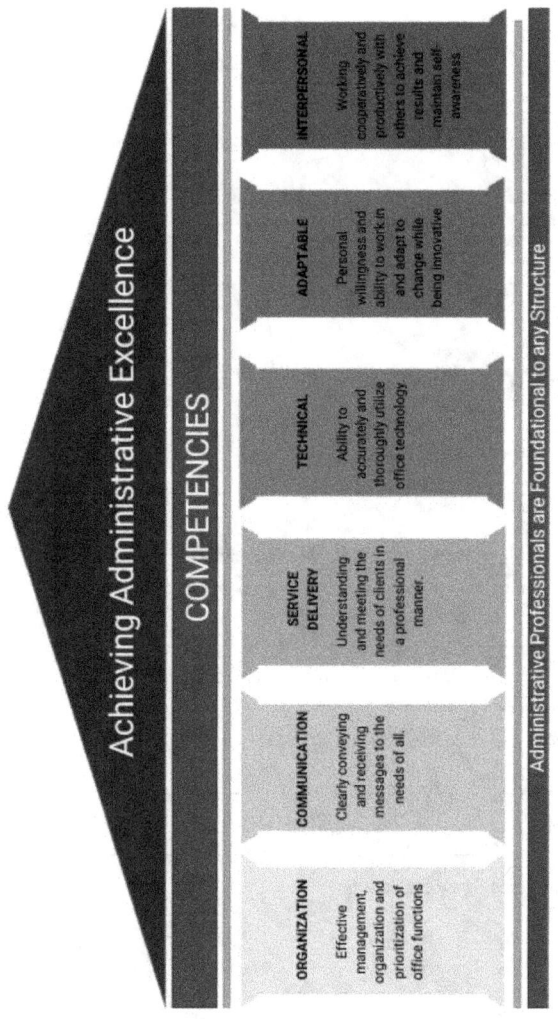

Source: Pillars of Excellence, Carol Walsh, 2022

Appendix 2 - Sample Charter Template

Name of Community:	
Name of Sponsor(s):	
CoP Lead(s):	
Organization Business Unit:	
Community Purpose Statement:	
Community Objectives: *(Objectives needed to support the organizational goals which may aim to improve key performance indicators (KPIs)*	
Community Scope:	
In Scope:	Not in Scope:
Business Goals and Benefits: *(How does this meet organizational goals and provide benefit to the organization?)*	
Goals:	Benefits:
Roles and Resources: *(Team Members/Expertise)*	
Performance Metrics: *(How community success will be evaluated.)*	
Critical Success Factors and Barriers: *(What needs to happen to ensure community success, and what challenges might the community need to overcome to meet its goals.)*	
Success Factors:	Barriers:

Appendix 3: Checklist to Evaluate Communities of Practice[7]

This simple checklist can be used to evaluate a community of practice. APQC recommends using the list to assess community readiness prior to launch as well as to monitor existing communities and identify opportunities for improvement.

Questions	Y/N	Comments
1. Does your community have a compelling, clear business value proposition?		
2. Does your community have a dedicated, skilled leader and/or facilitator?		
3. Does your community have a coherent, comprehensive knowledge map of key content?		
4. Does your community have an easy-to-follow knowledge-sharing process?		
5. Does your community have appropriate technology to facilitate knowledge exchange?		
6. Does your community have communication and training plans for members and others?		
7. Does your community have a current, updated roster of participants?		
8. Does your community have several key metrics to show business impact?		
9. Does your community have a recognition process for participants?		

[7] Checklist to Evaluate Communities of Practice, American Productivity & Quality Center (APQC), https://www.apqc.org/resource-library/resource-listing/checklist-evaluate-communities-practice, 2018 – Public Content

Questions	Y/N	Comments
10. Does your community have an agenda of topics/problems to solve for the next three to six months?		

Appendix 4 - Sample Framework Response

Goal: Administrative professionals have skills and knowledge required to excel in their jobs and are part of a mutual support network that contributes to their success.

Outcomes (big picture benefit to admins)	Outputs (What concrete items will let us know we are working towards the outcome?)	Activities (What do we need to do to generate outputs?)
The CoP Resources and supports are accessed and used by administrative professionals.	Promotional materials are developed, distributed, and monitored for all available resources to current and new admins.	1. Create a Communication / Promotions Committee. 2. Distribute a quarterly newsletter to promote all activities. 3. Deliver presentations to various audiences.

Appendix 5 - Sample Framework Tracking Form

Outcome:		
Task:		Status ☐ Not Started ☐ In progress ☐ Completed
Date Started	Due Date	Date completed
Comments		

REFERENCES

1. 148 Keeping Momentum in Remote Communities of Practice, Podcast, June 26, 2017, 148 - Keeping Momentum in Remote Communities of Practice - Collaboration Superpowers.

2. Alberta Health Services, Achieving Administrative Excellence Community of Practice.

3. https://extranet.ahsnet.ca/teams/cop/aae/sitepages/home.aspx

4. American Productivity & Quality Center (APQC). A Well-Designed Launch Process Positions Communities of Practice for Success. (2018) A Well-Designed Launch Process. Positions Communities of Practice for Success | APQC

5. American Productivity & Quality Center (APQC). Community of Practice Charter Template. (2018). https://www.apqc.org/knowledge-base/documents/community-practice-charter-template

6. American Productivity & Quality Center (APQC). Four Proven Strategies to Evaluate Communities of Practice. 2018. https://www.apqc.org/knowledge-base/documents/four-proven-strategies-evaluate-communities-practice

7. American Productivity & Quality Center (APQC). Key Measures for Communities of Practice and Networks. 2018. https://www.apqc.org/knowledge-base/documents/key-measures-communities-practice-and-networks

8. American Productivity & Quality Center (APQC). Performance Improvement Team Charter. 2018. https://www.apqc.org/knowledgebase/documents/performance-improvement-team-charter

9. American Productivity & Quality Center (APQC). The Dos and Don'ts of Community Charters. 2018. https://www.apqc.org/knowledge-base/documents/dos-and-donts-community-charters

10. American Productivity & Quality Center (APQC). The Dos and Don'ts of Community Charters. 2018. https://www.apqc.org/knowledgebase/download/414422/K08506_Five%20Classic%20Engagement%20Strategies%20for%20CoPs.pdf

11. American Productivity & Quality Center (APQC). The Dos and Don'ts of Community Charters. 2018. https://www.apqc.org/knowledge-base/download/414423/K08507_Formal%20and%20Informal%20Ways%20to%20Recognize%20CoP%20Contributions.pdf

12. American Productivity & Quality Center (APQC). The Dos and Don'ts of Community Charters. 2018. https://www.apqc.org/knowledgebase/download/410346/K08314_CoPs%20Should%20Be%20Designed%20to%20Promote%20Employee%20Learningv2.pdf

13. Association of Administrative Professional Staff at UBC. Professional Development Communities of Practice. https://aaps.ubc.ca/ 2019.

14. Centers for Disease Control. Plan Communities of Practice Charter Template. https://www.cdc.gov/phcommunities/docs/plan_cop_charter_template.doc: 2019.

15. Etienne Wegner, Richard McDermott, William M. Snyder. "A Guide to Managing Knowledge: Cultivating Communities of Practice". 2002. https://hbswk.hbs.edu/archive/cultivating-communities-of-practice-a-guide-to-managingknowledge-seven-principles-for-cultivating-communities-of-practice and http://www.cpcoaching.it/wpcontent/uploads/2012/05/WengerCPC.pdf

16. Etienne Wegner, Richard McDermott, William M. Snyder. "A Guide to Managing Knowledge: Cultivating Communities of Practice". 2002. Harvard Business School Press. Boston Massachusetts.

https://hbswk.hbs.edu/archive/cultivating-communities-of-practice-a-guide-to-managing-knowledge-seven-principles-for-cultivating-communities-of-practice, W:2019

17. Etienne Wenger, Richard McDermott and William Snider, Cultivating Communities of Practice: A Guide to Managing Knowledge - Seven Principles for Cultivating Communities of Practice, Harvard Business School, Working Knowledge – Business Research for Business Leaders, 3/25/2002. https://hbswk.hbs.edu/archive/cultivating-communities-of-practice-a-guide-to-managing-knowledge-seven-principles-for-cultivating-communities-of-practice.

18. Etienne Wenger. Cultivating communities of practice, a quick start-up guide. https://wenger-trayner.com/project/community-of-practice-start-up-guide/.2019

19. Etienne Wenger-Trayner and Beverly Wenger-Trayner. Introduction to communities of practice: A brief overview of the concept and its uses. 2015. https://wenger-trayner.com/introduction-to-communities-of-practice.

20. Fontaine, M., & Prusak, L. 2004. Keeping communities of practice afloat: Understanding and fostering roles in communities. DOI:10.1093/0195165128.003.0008

21. George S. Gotto IV, Ann Turnbull, Jean Ann Summers, and Martha Blue-Banning. Rehabilitation Research and Training Centre on Policies Affecting Families and Children with Disabilities. Beach Center on Disability. Community of Practice Development Manual. http://ktdrr.org/resources/rush/copmanual/CoP_Manual.pdf. 2019.

22. Gonçalves, Luis. OrganisationalMastery.com. Communities of Practice: Everything You Need to Know. March 11, 2019. https://www.organisationalmastery.com/communities-of-practice. 2019.

23. Griffith University. Guidelines for Establishing Communities of Practice. https://policies.griffith.edu.au/pdf/Guidelines%20for%20Establishing%20Communities%20of%20Practice.pdf

24. Igor Pyrko, Viktor Dorfier and Colin Eden. Thinking together: What makes Communities of Practice Work? University of Strathclyde, UK. SAGE, Human Relations; Studies towards the integration of the Social Sciences. PMCID: PMC5305036 August 26, 2016, doi: 10.1177/0018726716661040; Hum Relat: April 2017 70(4): 289-409. Access website: https://journals.sagepub.com/doi/full/10.1177/0018726716661040. 2019

25. LaserFiche.com. Create a Community of Practice in Your Organization. https://www.laserfiche.com/ecmblog/create-a-community-of-practice-in-your-organization: 2019.

26. Lesser, E., & Prusak, L. (Eds.), Creating value with knowledge: Insights from the IBM Institute for Business Value (pp. 124-133). New York, NY: Oxford University Press. http://doi.org/10.1093/0195165128.001.0001

27. Matthew Luxton. Communities of Practice – Behaviours and Benefits. August 12, 2011. Elizabeth Goodman Blog. https://elisabethgoodman.wordpress.com/2011/08/12/communities-of-practice-%e2%80%93-behaviours-and-benefits/. 2019.

28. Melanie Barwick. Canadian Knowledge Exchange and Transfer Community of Practice. September 25, 2008. www.ktecop.ca/wordpress/wpcontent/uploads/developing_a_community_of_practice_ppt: 2019.

29. National Library of Medicine, Virtual communities of practice: can they support the prevention agenda in public health? https://www.bing.com/ck/a?!&&p=586ab4e2fe00c149JmltdHM9MTY2NTM2MDAwMCZpZ3VpZD0wYTUzNWE2ZS0wZDRmLTZlNjItM2Y4ZC01NDgyMGNlYzZmNjEmaW5zaWQ9NTE4Ng&ptn=3&hsh=3&fclid=0a535a6e-0d4f-6e62-3f8d-54820cec6f61&psq=Virtual+communities+of+practice%3a+can+they+support+the+prevention+agenda+in+public+health%3f&u=a1aHR0cHM6Ly93d3cucmVzZWFyY2hnYXRlLm5ldC9wdWJsaWNhdGlvbi8yODEwODExMDdfVmlydHVhbF9jb21tdW5pdGllc19vZl9wcmFjdGljZV9jYW5fdGhleV9zdXBwb3J0X3RoZV9wcmV2ZW50aW9uX2FnZW5kYV9pbl9wdWJsaWNfaGVhbHRo&ntb=1

30. Nelson, Lisa. What are the Benefits of a Community of Practice (CoP) | Graphic Recording, Sketchnotes - Washington, DC.

https://seeincolors.com/what-are-the-benefits-of-a-community-of-practice-cop. 2021.

31. Orlala Wentink, The role of a sponsor in a virtual community of practice (Module 4, ISTE-CS 4), March 15, 2018. http://owentink.org/the-role-of-a-sponsor-in-a-virtual-community-of-practice-module-4-iste-cs-4. 2019.

32. Pappas, Christopher. Top 10 tips To Create a Corporate Learning Community of Practice. September 16, 2014. https://elearningindustry.com/top-10-tips-create-corporate-learning-community-of-practice. 2019.

33. Seven Principles for Cultivating Communities of Practice HBSWK Pub. Date: Mar 25, 2002. https://www.clearwatervic.com.au/resource-library/publications-and-reports/7-principles-of-community-of-practice.php.

34. Smith, Jenny, and Sherman Teresa A. Virtual Communities of Practice: 9 Tips to Engage Participants. April 27, 2018. eLearning Industry. https://elearningindustry.com/virtual-communities-of-practice-9-tips-engage-participants .

35. Therese Sullivan, Contributing Editor – AutomatedBuildings.com. Communities of Practice in Building Automation. March 2019. http://www.automatedbuildings.com/editors/tsullivan.html.

36. Virtual communities of practice: can they support the prevention agenda in public health? - PMC (nih.gov). (2015) https://doi.org/10.5210%2Fojphi.v7i2.6031.

37. Wenger, Etienne. Cultivating communities of practice, a quick start-up guide. https://wenger-trayner.com/project/community-of-practice-start-up-guide/.

38. Wenger-Trayner, Team BE. Communities versus networks? December 28, 2011. https://wegnertrayner.com/resources/communities-versus-networks.

39. Wenger-Trayner, Team BE. Communities versus networks? December 28, 2011. https://wegner-trayner.com/resources/communities-versus-networks: W:2019.

40. *SAFe®*, Scaled Agile Framework, Communities of Practice. https://www.scaledagileframework.com/ communities-of-practice. 2022.

41. Public Health Ontario, Focus on: Logic Model –A Planning and Evaluation Tool, website: https://www.publichealthontario.ca/-/media/documents/f/2016/focus-on-logicmodel.pdf#:~:text= A%20logic%20model%20is%20a%20visual%20illustration%20of,concurrently%20with%20logic%20models%20is%20theory%20of%20change. Accessed: 2019.

42. TolaData, The Results Framework, website: https://www.toladata.com/docs/knowledge-base/indicator-workflow/what-is-a-results-framework/, Accessed 2021.

www.ingramcontent.com/pod-product-compliance
Lightning Source LLC
Chambersburg PA
CBHW071519220526
45472CB00003B/1084